Delegation Skills

Delegation Skills

BRUCE B. TEPPER

Business Skills Express Series

IRWIN
Professional Publishing

MIRROR PRESS

Burr Ridge, Illinois
New York, New York
Boston, Massachusetts

© RICHARD D. IRWIN, INC., 1994

Mirror Press: David R. Helmstadter
                             Carla F. Tishler

Editor-in-chief: Jeffrey A. Krames
Project editor: Jane Lightell
Production manager: Diane Palmer
Designer: Jeanne M. Rivera
Art manager: Kim Meriwether
Compositor: Alexander Graphics
Typeface: 12/14 Criterion
Printer: Malloy Lithographing, Inc.

Library of Congress Cataloging-in-Publication Data

Tepper, Bruce B.
    Delegation skills / Bruce B. Tepper.
        p.   cm. — (The Business skills express series)
    ISBN 0-7863-0148-1
        1. Delegation of authority.   I. Title.   II. Series.
    HD50.T46   1994
    658.4'02—dc20   93–29257

Printed in the United States of America
1 2 3 4 5 6 7 8 9 0 ML 0 9 8 7 6 5 4 3

PREFACE

Delegation is a problem for new supervisors, new managers, and experienced professionals alike. It is one of the greatest challenges we face in supervising others.

If you are new to supervision or management, you must learn a number of seemingly overwhelming tasks. Delegation is one of those tasks often put aside to be dealt with in the future because it is difficult to accomplish and carries with it many emotional implications.

Delegation is a skill that can be learned and developed. It is a skill that is critical to your growth as a supervisor or manager. You must know how to delegate if you want to have time to do your job properly and to motivate your subordinates to do their very best.

The easiest way to learn any skill, like delegation, is to break it down into its components and deal with each one separately. This book does just that. New supervisors or managers will gain helpful insights and ideas on setting up their own programs of delegating work. Seasoned veterans will learn some new ideas and have their efforts to be better supervisors reinforced.

Delegation is one of the most valuable tools available to make your job a success. It can bring you greater loyalty from subordinates and senior management. Good delegation skills can go a long way in helping you reach your own personal and business objectives.

Bruce B. Tepper

ABOUT THE AUTHOR

Bruce B. Tepper, a San Francisco-based associate of R.W. Joselyn & Associates specializes in management & supervision skills, customer service and sales training. As a consultant and speaker, his clients have included Holiday Inn's Inc, Continental Airlines, the American Society of Travel Agents, the American Automobile Association and American Express.

As a member of the National Speakers Association, the Academy of Professional Consultants and Advisors, Mr. Tepper is a Certified Professional Consultant (CPC). He is an accomplished author, speaker and instructor at San Francisco State University and Golden Gate University. Mr. Tepper holds an M.B.A., and an M.A. in Education.

ABOUT IRWIN PROFESSIONAL PUBLISHING

Irwin Professional Publishing is the nation's premier publisher of business books. As a Times Mirror company, we work closely with Times Mirror training organizations, including Zenger-Miller, Inc., Learning International, Inc., and Kaset International to serve the training needs of business and industry.

About the Business Skills Express Series

This expanding series of authoritative, concise, and fast-paced books delivers high-quality training on key business topics at a remarkably affordable cost. The series will help managers, supervisors, and frontline personnel in organizations of all sizes and types hone their business skills while enhancing job performance and career satisfaction.

Business Skills Express books are ideal for employee seminars, independent self-study, on-the-job training, and classroom-based instruction. Express books are also convenient-to-use references at work.

CONTENTS

Self-Assessment

The following self-assessment will help you to determine how sharp your delegation skills are and will suggest areas where improvements can be made. Using the following key, circle the number next to each statement that reflects how often you identify with the statement. Score yourself at the end of the self-assessment.

4 = Always

3 = Usually

2 = Sometimes

1 = Rarely

0 = Never

1. I make a point of not doing work assigned to employees.   0 1 2 3 4

2. I give clear directions regarding tasks that need to be done.   0 1 2 3 4

3. I do not feel threatened by good employees.   0 1 2 3 4

4. My sense of influence and success comes from the success of my subordinates.   0 1 2 3 4

5. I feel in control—even with projects I've delegated to others.   0 1 2 3 4

6. I feel confident about my direction and role as a supervisor.   0 1 2 3 4

7. I trust my subordinates to do a good job.   0 1 2 3 4

8. I take the time to teach my subordinates how to do tasks I have delegated.   0 1 2 3 4

9. I believe that delegating as many tasks as possible is in everyone's best interest.   0 1 2 3 4

10. I recognize the difference between being a supervisor and performing the tasks my employees perform.   0 1 2 3 4

11. I feel confident leading and directing others.   0 1 2 3 4

12. I am patient in allowing employees to complete tasks and to learn from their mistakes.   0 1 2 3 4

13. I give employees additional time to do a task correctly if it isn't done correctly the first time, rather than take the assignments away from the employees to do them myself.   0 1 2 3 4

14. Before delegating work, I break each task down into its basic components to see what skills will be needed.   0 1 2 3 4

15. I make sure employees have adequate training to perform each task.   0 1 2 3 4

16. I allow adequate time for employees to perform each task.   0 1 2 3 4

17. I examine obstacles employees may face in performing each task.   0 1 2 3 4

18. I try to match tasks to employee personality traits, thinking styles, and capabilities.   0 1 2 3 4

19. I do a profile on each employee and his or her capabilities.   0 1 2 3 4

20. I provide written instructions to employees for each new task they are to perform.   0 1 2 3 4

21. I review the instructions and details of the task and make sure the employee understands what is required.   0 1 2 3 4

22. I have contingency plans for delegated tasks to make sure the tasks get done.   0 1 2 3 4

23. I have developed and implemented an evaluation plan to monitor how well employees do with each task.   0 1 2 3 4

24. I encourage employees to make their own decisions and to solve problems related to new tasks.   0 1 2 3 4

25. I encourage employees to set their own performance objectives.   0 1 2 3 4

26. I maintain a very supportive posture for all of my subordinates.   0 1 2 3 4

27. I avoid harsh criticism of an employee's performance of new tasks.   0 1 2 3 4

28. I solicit feedback from employees on how they feel they are doing with new tasks.   0 1 2 3 4

29. I try to determine employee motivational needs when delegating tasks.   0 1 2 3 4

30. I enlist the support of my supervisor or manager for the delegation plans I implement.   0 1 2 3 4

31. I treat delegation as a productivity maximizer and as a method of developing employee skills.   0 1 2 3 4

32. I see my role as that of a general contractor or conductor; I see the big picture while orchestrating the activities of others.   0 1 2 3 4

33. I try to challenge my subordinates to extend their own capabilities.   0 1 2 3 4

34. I am open and receptive to new ways to handle old tasks that may come from my employees.   0 1 2 3 4

35. I believe that delegation is an essential element of good management, and it is important to me, my employees, my supervisor, and our customers.   0 1 2 3 4

Score Yourself

Total the number of points you have circled for all 35 statements.

Scoring 110 points or more means you are pretty comfortable with your role as a supervisor/manager and understand and accept the need to delegate work in performing your role. Although there is always room for improvement, you are close to being the kind of supervisor motivated employees like to work for. This book will help reinforce the skills you are using effectively.

A score of 80 to 109 points means you accept the need to delegate work and try to do so. Some weaknesses remain that need a little extra attention. This book will help you to strengthen those weaknesses.

Less than 80 points indicates that you are a relatively new supervisor/manager just beginning to delegate work or that you are battling obstacles to delegation. This book will give you the skills you need to become an effective delegator. In the process you will become a better supervisor or manager.

Good luck!

Delegation Skills

CHAPTER

1 | Why Work Should Be Delegated

This chapter will help you to:

- Appreciate the need to delegate work.
- Understand the impact of delegation on your supervision and management effectiveness.
- Recognize how important delegation is to your subordinates.

Tomás García is one of the hardest-working people employed by a tax consulting firm. He believes that his diligence and attention to detail are the main reasons he has been promoted to supervisor in the marketing department. Tomás has always been the top performer in *every category*, but now he is concerned about staying on top of the workload and maintaining the kind of quality that is necessary. He also is concerned about his new management duties and how he can handle everything.

As a supervisor, Tomás has a staff reporting to him. He is concerned that they will not be able to do their jobs, so he is inclined to do everything himself. That way he knows the tasks will be done correctly. Tomás says, "There just isn't time to teach the staff all they need to know." He feels he can delegate work later on when he is more established. ■

Questions to Consider

1. Is Tomás likely to succeed if he does not delegate job tasks and instead performs all the tasks himself? Why or why not?

_____

_____

_____

2. How might Tomás overcome his fear of delegation?

_____

_____

_____

WHY DELEGATING WORK IS SO IMPORTANT

One of the most critical keys to successful management and supervision is the ability to delegate work to others. Delegation of work offers major advantages to the supervisor, employees, and the company.

   1. As a supervisor or manager, you will have time to manage, which is a job totally different from any job done by the people who work for you.

   2. You will have time to develop management and supervision skills that will add to your productivity and, consequently, improve the company's performance.

   3. You will help develop other people and improve their skills.

   4. You will be able to identify talent and ability more clearly among your subordinates by allowing them to become more involved in a greater variety of tasks.

5. You will demonstrate respect and appreciation for those who report to you. By delegating work, you let your employees know that you trust them and want them to be successful.

Do You Need To Delegate?

Take this brief quiz to determine how pressing your need is to delegate work.

		Yes	No
1.	Do you feel overwhelmed with work?	____	____
2.	Do you find yourself working too many hours?	____	____
3.	Do you leave tasks unfinished?	____	____
4.	Do you fail to meet deadlines?	____	____
5.	Is the quality of work from your department as good as it should be?	____	____
6.	Do your employees regularly ask for additional assignments or more responsibility?	____	____
7.	Are you having difficulty organizing assignments and tasks?	____	____

If you answered yes to more than two of these questions, you probably are having major problems doing your job as a supervisor or manager.

THE EFFECTIVE SUPERVISOR/MANAGER

Management skills are distinct from frontline skills and tasks. In many businesses it is common practice to promote the best "task performer" to manager. Frequently, there is an attitude of benign neglect: if you are good at your job, you probably will be a great manager or supervisor. Unfortunately, the skills needed to supervise are totally different from those required to perform job-specific tasks. If you fail to delegate work, you will never learn and apply the necessary skills of supervision and management.

1

Are You a Good Supervisor/Manager?

Take a moment to evaluate your supervision skills. Complete each statement by checking the appropriate blank.

	Excellent	Good	Poor (Needs Improvement)
1. My ability to give clear direction to other people is	_____	_____	_____
2. My management skills are	_____	_____	_____
3. My leadership skills are	_____	_____	_____
4. My decision-making skills are	_____	_____	_____
5. My ability to introduce and handle changes is	_____	_____	_____
6. My ability to manage my time effectively	_____	_____	_____
7. My ability to use praise and criticism is	_____	_____	_____
8. My ability to set goals and objectives and meet them is	_____	_____	_____
9. My ability to generate a positive attitude among my subordinates is	_____	_____	_____
10. My ability to focus on the big picture and not get bogged down in doing the job of my employees is	_____	_____	_____

These statements reflect the essential elements of supervision and management. If you are not good or excellent in every category, failure to delegate work may be one of the main reasons. Delegation frees up your time and allows you to focus on what you were hired to do: manage and supervise.

DELEGATION AND YOUR SUBORDINATES

Delegation is also important to the people who work for you.

- It demonstrates your faith and trust in their ability.
- It allows them to develop and improve their skills.
- It creates greater involvement for them in their company.
- It is a sign of respect for their capabilities.
- It helps you to evaluate them on a much broader basis. You see their potential in many areas.
- It builds morale. Think back to the days before you were a supervisor. Didn't you seek out tasks to demonstrate your capabilities and sense of responsibility? Don't deny that aspect of the job to the people who work for you.

Take the following quiz, duplicate it, and give copies to your subordinates. Ask each of them to complete the quiz anonymously and return it to you. At the same time, take the quiz yourself and see how closely the answers of your subordinates match your own.

After you and your group have taken the quiz, step back for a moment. How did you do? How did your employees do? How far apart are the opinions of you and your employees on your delegation skills and willingness to delegate work?

1

Supervisor Evaluation

	Always	Sometimes	Never
1. The supervisor is afraid to delegate projects or work.	_____	_____	_____
2. The supervisor is a perfectionist and doesn't tolerate errors. Consequently, the supervisor tends to take over tasks that aren't being done perfectly.	_____	_____	_____
3. The supervisor is impatient and likes to do the job to make sure it is completed on time.	_____	_____	_____
4. The supervisor doesn't seem to trust employees to do the job properly.	_____	_____	_____
5. The supervisor feels threatened if employees excel at their jobs.	_____	_____	_____
6. The supervisor does not adequately explain the job that needs to be done.	_____	_____	_____
7. The supervisor assigns jobs that are too difficult.	_____	_____	_____
8. The supervisor delegates only the most meaningless work.	_____	_____	_____

Chapter 1 Checkpoints

✓ You must believe that the need to delegate work is crucial.

✓ Subordinates must be trusted to do their jobs properly.

✓ You must be patient enough to teach subordinates what they will need to know to do their jobs properly.

✓ Be sure to delegate work to give yourself the chance to learn new supervisory management skills.

2 | Overcoming Obstacles to Delegation

This chapter will help you to:

- Understand the obstacles to delegating work.
- Overcome delegation obstacles and begin the process of delegation.

Rosemary Weissgarten has been a supervisor at a publishing company for several months. She is becoming more firmly established in her job but still does most of the work herself. By doing the work rather than delegating it, she ensures quality and, quite frankly, she enjoys many of the tasks she has to perform.

Intellectually, Rosemary knows she must make a more concerted effort to delegate tasks. But emotionally, it is very difficult for her to do so. ''When you've done certain types of work for a long period of time, you get used to doing it yourself,'' says Rosemary. ■

■ Questions to Consider

1. How can Rosemary let go of the tasks she no longer needs to perform?

_____

_____

_____

2. How can Rosemary ensure that the tasks she does so well will be performed as well by her subordinates?

_____

_____

_____

UNDERSTANDING THE OBSTACLES

Supervisors and managers find it difficult to delegate work to other people for several reasons.

   1. After working in a job for some time, much of your sense of confidence and, for that matter, power, comes from your knowledge of the job. If other people do your work, you truly feel a sense of loss. Consequently, when moving into a supervisory or managerial job, you will have a strong desire to continue doing the work you did before becoming a supervisor.

   2. You may sense a loss of control. Someone else will do the tasks you used to do, and they may do them better! They might become the recognized authority in the office, just as you might have been in the past. Recall Tomás García from Chapter 1. Prior to being promoted, he was the best at his work. He may experience a true sense of loss if someone else learns his former tasks and usurps his expertise.

   3. You may sense a loss of direction and focus. When you begin work as a supervisor or manager, you must learn new tasks. In a sense, you are starting all over. Your confidence level may drop because you are a "student" again. After becoming very proficient at a job, you may find it difficult to walk away from it.

4. You may lose your sense of accomplishment. When you perform tasks and complete them, you often sense great satisfaction. As a supervisor, you oversee others who get the sense of accomplishment instead.

Take the following quiz to determine your sensitivity to these issues.

Are You Able To Let Go?

	Always	Sometimes	Never
1. Since I'm responsible for the results, I have an obligation to handle tasks others may not be able to do.	_____	_____	_____
2. I find it very difficult to trust others to do things as well as I do.	_____	_____	_____
3. I find it difficult to trust others to do things as quickly as I do.	_____	_____	_____
4. It bothers me to see someone else do my old job differently from the way I did it.	_____	_____	_____
5. Without doing my old job, I feel somewhat lost.	_____	_____	_____
6. I enjoyed the tasks on my old job more than the new tasks I'm supposed to do.	_____	_____	_____
7. I find it emotionally draining to give up what I've done for so long.	_____	_____	_____

Even one "always" is too many on this quiz, although an always answer for statement 6 may be understandable for a short period of time.

In time, you will build confidence as you learn new tasks. However, there is no reason to wait. By facing the change squarely and moving quickly into learning new tasks, you can accelerate your elimination of these sensitive issues.

OVERCOMING OBSTACLES

Several steps can help you overcome the obstacles to delegation.

1. Accept delegation as inevitable. Stop fighting it. You cannot do your job properly as a supervisor or manager without delegating work to others.

2. Develop your new skills of supervision. The books in the Business Skills Express series are designed to help you do that. Focus on how quickly you can learn new skills and how quickly you can set up a delegation plan as described in Chapter 5 of this book.

3. Think about when you first started your last job. The fear of the unknown and the knowledge that you had much to learn undoubtedly were part of your thoughts. You mastered the old job and did it well or very likely you would not have become a supervisor. Your new challenges are much the same. Don't let new responsibilities intimidate you. Break down the tasks and learn them one by one. In time, you will find that supervision will be just as rewarding, if not more so, as your old job.

4. Take any additional steps. You may find it necessary to learn more about supervision and management and to increase your comfort level with your new role.

Complete the following delegation progress chart and set a timetable for completing every step.

Delegation Progress

Task/Goal   **Date Completed**

1. I have complete confidence in my ability to lead
others.   _____

2. I have developed the necessary skills to supervise and direct the activity of others.   _____

3. I have identified five tasks that I used to do that
should now be done by others. I am comfortable
delegating the following tasks that I used to do: _____

    a. _____   _____

    b. _____   _____

(continued)

Delegation Progress (concluded)

	Task/Goal	Date Completed
c.	_____	_____
d.	_____	_____
e.	_____	_____

4. I have identified three key tasks I must learn, and I will learn them by the date listed. _____

a.	_____	_____
b.	_____	_____
c.	_____	_____

5. I have overcome all fears of being shown up by subordinates or replacements on my old job. _____

6. I am able to teach others without jumping in and finishing tasks. _____

7. I have the patience to allow others to make mistakes and learn their job. _____

There is no correct numerical score. Your objectives are to:

- Step into your new role and supervise others. Don't do the tasks yourself.

- Step back and allow others to develop and learn even if they make mistakes.

- Step up and start learning new skills that will help you do your job better and enhance your career.

Overcoming the obstacles to delegation requires a mind-set that permits you to grow. You must think of yourself as a new person with new responsibilities. Do not let fear or insecurity hold you back. You can develop new skills as you have done before. Delegation does not come naturally. Make it a part of your conscious thoughts until it becomes a little more routine.

Chapter 2 Checkpoints

✓ Accept your role as a supervisor and make a conscious effort not to do tasks others should do.

✓ Develop an attitude of wanting to develop the skills of others without stepping in and doing their jobs for them.

✓ Recognize the sense of loss that can occur when delegating work, but welcome the challenge of learning new tasks.

✓ Accept the fact that others may do your old job differently than you, better than you, or both.

✓ Recognize that your new role of supervising others includes developing the talents of your subordinates.

CHAPTER

3 | Choosing the Right Tasks to Delegate

This chapter will help you to:

- Review your areas of responsibility.
- Determine which tasks are most suited to delegation.
- Develop a priority list of tasks to be delegated.

James Watson has just been appointed to the position of supervisor in the menswear department of a large department store. His responsibilities include supervising a staff of 15 people who cover all the hours the store is open, selecting merchandise to display and where to display it (except for promotions developed by the store's marketing and advertising department), and reviewing inventory to make recommendations to management on trends and client interests. James knows that it is essential to delegate some of the work to his assistants, but he is not sure where to begin. ■

■ Questions to Consider

1. Which tasks should James control? Why?

_____

_____

_____

2. Which tasks should James delegate? Why?

_____

_____

_____

AREAS OF RESPONSIBILITY

Let's begin by separating the issues of responsibility and delegation. James may choose to delegate any variety of tasks he wishes. However, he still, remains responsible for their completion.

One obstacle to delegation that was not discussed in Chapter 2 is the fear of being responsible for someone else's work and having that work fail to live up to expectations. Supervisors and managers cannot delegate responsibility for work under their direction. Consequently, James must choose his tasks carefully to make sure they will be done properly. In many cases, he should continually review the work of others to make sure it is up to acceptable standards.

Getting Started in Task Selection

Choosing tasks to delegate begins with breaking down a job into small components. The best place to start is with your job description. If you have a formal job description, list the tasks described, then break them down into their smallest possible components.

The following breakdowns work for James Watson:

3

Supervision of Staff
- Determine work schedules.
- Conduct employee reviews.
- Provide ongoing skills and sales training/support.
- Mediate employee disputes.
- Assign work.
- Cover counters as a backup salesperson in busy times.
- Review daily invoices for commission reports.
- Motivate salespeople to work harder.
- Handle customer service problems/complaints.

Merchandising
- Review each shelf and display area to make sure they are adequately stocked and neatly arranged.
- Replace display stock as needed or rearrange displays as necessary.
- Review displays for appeal and reorganize as necessary.
- Maintain cleanliness of display areas.
- Make sure all marketing department displays are set up and maintained.

Inventory Control
- Review invoices on a daily basis to make sure control tags have been removed from garments and attached to the store copy of the receipt.
- Complete the daily inventory report, listing items sold by category.
- Check stock daily to make sure adequate supplies of popular items have been ordered from the store's warehouse and are in the stockroom.

- Complete the trend report for store buyers on items customers ask for that are unavailable or out of stock and on items that are moving up or down in popularity.

In looking through James's list, there are a number of items that clearly can be delegated (for example, checking stock daily). This list is a starting point for James to determine where to delegate.

Now it's your turn. Complete the chart below using *your* job description as a basis for general categories. Under the General Categories column, list your primary responsibilities. There probably will be less than four or five. (James's were supervision of staff, merchandising, and inventory control.) In the right-hand column, list the specific tasks in a manner similar to those on James's list.

Task Selection and Responsibilities

General Categories   **Specific Elements**

_____   _____
_____   _____
_____   _____
_____   _____
_____   _____
_____   _____
_____   _____
_____   _____
_____   _____
_____   _____

WHICH TASKS ARE BEST SUITED TO DELEGATION?

Now add a third column in the right-hand margin next to each individual task and label it "Delegate." In this column, write a yes or no after answering the following questions:

1. Is the task one that logically should and could be done by someone else? (That is, the task is not clearly a management/supervision task such as conducting employee reviews.)

2. Do I feel comfortable turning this task over to the right person, knowing I'm still responsible for the results? (Remember, you cannot do everything yourself, so it will be necessary to delegate work.)

3. Are any of my staff trained and/or capable of handling this task?

4. Will the person chosen to handle this task have adequate time to perform it effectively?

5. Can I present this task as an important one to make sure the individual who carries it out does it properly?

Developing A Priority List

Not every task that should be delegated can be delegated all the time.

- There may not be anyone qualified to do the task when you need it done.

- It may be necessary to provide training, which you may not have time to provide immediately.

- Some tasks are seasonal and do not require permanent work assignments.

With these thoughts in mind, complete the following table, listing in the left-hand column each task that you have decided can be delegated under the right circumstances. Next to each task, list any obstacles to delegating the task right now. In the right-hand column, list your target date for delegating the task—one that gives you time to overcome obstacles listed in the middle column.

Priority List: Tasks to Delegate

Task	Obstacles	Implementation Date
_____	_____	_____
_____	_____	_____
_____	_____	_____

(continued)

Priority List: Tasks to Delegate (concluded)

Task	Obstacles	Implementation Date
_____	_____	_____
_____	_____	_____
_____	_____	_____
_____	_____	_____
_____	_____	_____
_____	_____	_____
_____	_____	_____

Delegating Work to Your Supervisor

In some cases, it makes sense to delegate work upward to your manager or supervisor.

If a situation occurs that may involve procedural change that could affect other departments, it may be more logical to delegate the decision and implementation to your supervisor. He or she may be in a better position to get things done more quickly.

If you feel you can improve your boss's comfort level by involving him or her, do so. Like you, your boss may suffer from anxieties about delegating work and responsibility.

If delegation of certain assignments is likely to meet resistance, you may want the extra authority your boss's position brings to the table. Be careful though: you do not want to risk undermining your own authority as a supervisor.

If you feel apprehensive about delegating a task, you may want your boss to make the decision for you. Again, be careful. You do not want to appear weak or indecisive.

Chapter 3 Checkpoints

✓ Create a clear and concise job description for your position.

✓ Break down each main area of responsibility into small tasks.

✓ Review each task and determine whether you must do it or whether it can be done by someone else.

✓ Create an implementation timetable for every task that can be delegated.

✓ Note tasks that may involve policy changes so you can enlist the help of your supervisor or manager.

✓ Constantly evaluate each task to make sure it still is worth doing, and recommend eliminating tasks that are no longer necessary.

CHAPTER

4 | Delegating Tasks to the Right People

This chapter will help you to:

- Determine who is capable of handling delegated tasks.
- Select which tasks should be delegated to each of your subordinates.

The hotel reservations center where Sonia Owens works as a supervisor recently reorganized, giving her new areas of responsibility. She now supervises telephone operators handling inbound calls for two hotel chains; the operators are required to use different procedures for each chain.

The increased workload brought on by new responsibilities has convinced Sonia that she must delegate a number of tasks to handle her job efficiently. She has selected the tasks to be delegated; her problem now is to decide who is best suited to handle those tasks. ■

Questions to Consider

1. Why is Sonia's decision a difficult one to make?

_____

_____

_____

2. What steps can Sonia take to make her decision?

_____

_____

_____

DETERMINING WHO IS CAPABLE OF HANDLING DELEGATED TASKS

Theoretically, every employee should be capable of taking on additional responsibility as needed. Realistically, other considerations must be taken into account.

The first step in deciding whether or not a person is capable of handling a new assignment is to answer the following six questions:

1. Will the person have time to do the task? This is a basic question but one that must be considered. The supervisor must determine whether the task interferes with the subordinate's ability to do his or her primary job.

2. Does the person have the ability to do the task? If the task requires physical strength, a great aptitude for math, a highly creative mind, etc., the individual may not be up to handling the task.

3. Is the person trained to do the task? Even though an individual is capable of doing the work, he or she may not have the training to do it.

4. If the person lacks the skills to do the task, can he or she be taught those skills in a reasonable period of time?

5. Is the person generally reliable? In an ideal world, all of your employees are reliable, but in real life they may not be. Reliability can be a key factor if you need the task done in a timely manner.

6. Is the person seeking out new responsibility? One of the reasons for delegating work is to develop your employees. If for some reason individuals do not want additional responsibilities or duties, do not force extra tasks upon them. Try to find someone who will benefit from helping you.

Ideally, you can answer yes to all of these questions about delegating a task. In some situations, however, it may be absolutely necessary to delegate tasks when you cannot answer yes to all six questions. In such cases, be prepared to monitor closely the tasks you delegate. Do not wait until they are completed before checking progress.

At the hotel reservations center, Sonia is likely to be faced with having her employees handle calls for both hotel chains, not just one. Each chain's procedures may be very different, and her employees may not have been trained for both.

Sonia would be wise to consider reliability and willingness to help above some of the other characteristics. Most likely, the necessary skills can be taught fairly quickly and the employees should, in all cases, be capable of doing the work unless they are so busy in their present jobs that they have no more time.

MATCHING THE TASKS TO THE PEOPLE

Not everyone who works for you will be capable of doing every task you want to delegate to them. To help determine who is best suited, take each task and determine the skills and aptitudes necessary to do the job.

For each task you plan to delegate, complete the following chart. Circle those traits that are required for each task, and add to each category as appropriate. The results will give you a profile of what the task requires. You may want to make copies of this chart for future use.

Task Profile

TASK: _____

_____

Thinking Styles ☐
Quick decision making ☐
Creative thinking ☐
Ability to see the "big picture" ☐
Other: ☐

Personality Traits ☐
Patience ☐
Empathy and understanding ☐
Friendliness ☐
Sensitivity ☐
Intensive style ☐
Relaxed style ☐
Perseverance ☐
Forceful ☐
Individualistic ☐
Team player ☐
Other: ☐

Existing Abilities (that do not require time to ☐
learn or develop)
Physical strength ☐
Math aptitude ☐
Language aptitude (good communications skills) ☐
Manual dexterity ☐
Pleasant telephone voice/vocal skills ☐
Other: ☐

Other Categories and Requirements ☐

The next step is to match your employees to the task requirements. You want to determine who can do what.

Complete the following chart for each of your employees. Again, you may want to make extra copies.

Employee Profile

Employee Name _____

1. What adjectives describe this person's personality? (Forceful and decisive, timid and indecisive, etc.)

2. What is this person's style of thinking? (Creative and innovative, able to see the big picture of our company as a whole, good at implementing ideas of others, narrowly focused on his or her own job/department, etc.)

3. What special skills or aptitudes does this person possess? (Physical strength, a whiz at math, etc.)

Putting People and Tasks Together

The next step is a fairly obvious one: finding the best fit between the tasks and the people available. This is not a contest, however. While the best fit is always desirable, circumstances may cause you to select someone else. For example, you may have one person who is the best fit for every task you want to delegate. But it would not be reasonable or fair to assign all of those tasks to that person.

To create your delegation plan, you will need to put the attributes and skills that you have already identified into some sort of order for each task. Use the chart below to organize them.

4

Task—Employee Fit		
Task	**Attributes/ Skills Needed**	**Order of Importance***

---

*1 = highest need/essential

 2 = very useful

 3 = helpful but not vital

By now you have determined what skills each task requires, the order of importance of those skills, and the individuals best suited to handle those tasks.

Errors of Judgment: Who Is Capable of Doing What?

Don't be frustrated by mistakes and errors. Learn from them. Making judgments about the skills and abilities of subordinates may have to be done without complete information. That is one of the reasons it is important to know something about the people who work for you. It can help reduce, but not eliminate, errors in judgment. When errors are made, do not be afraid to correct your course and reevaluate the individual's ability to do a task.

Chapter 4 Checkpoints

✓ Identify all key tasks to be delegated.

✓ Determine the capability of each employee to take on new tasks.

✓ Determine the skills and aptitudes required for each task that you have decided to delegate.

✓ Determine each employee's skills and aptitudes in relation to the tasks you plan to delegate.

✓ Prioritize the skills required for each task you plan to delegate.

✓ Recognize the possibility for errors in judgment and review your appraisals regularly to make sure they are correct.

CHAPTER

5 | Creating and Using a Delegation Plan

This chapter will help you to:

- Establish a delegation plan.
- Put your plan into action.

William Jafir is a supervisor for an auto parts manufacturer. He has accepted the need to delegate many of the tasks he is responsible for handling. He has gone through his work carefully and identified and prioritized the tasks he is prepared to delegate. He also has taken a close look at his staff and has a pretty good idea of their capabilities, time limitations, and so on.

The challenge for William now is to get a plan up and running—to start assigning work in some logical fashion. William wants to install a program that will be accepted by his employees and ensure a reasonable balance of work for everyone. ■

▎ Questions to Consider

1. How should William go about creating his delegation plan?

_____

_____

_____

2. How can William gain the acceptance of his employees to the plan?

_____

_____

_____

ESTABLISHING A DELEGATION PLAN

To establish a delegation plan, look at your task list from Chapter 3. Determine how long each task takes you to complete, and consider whether each task might take longer for someone else to complete.

Determining How Much Time Is Needed

The best way to determine the amount of time needed to complete a task is to fill out a time log and track how much time you spend on the task. Unlike traditional time logs, you track only the total time needed, not when the activity occurs.

Set up the time log to cover a sufficient period of time. This depends on how often you perform each task. If each task is repeated within five days, a weekly log will be sufficient. You should be able to track most tasks within a month.

Time Log

TASK	TIME NEEDED TO COMPLETE	
	BY ME	BY EMPLOYEE
_____	_____	_____
_____	_____	_____
_____	_____	_____
_____	_____	_____
_____	_____	_____
_____	_____	_____
_____	_____	_____
_____	_____	_____
_____	_____	_____

After tracking your own tasks and time, estimate how long it will take your employees to complete the tasks. With some direction from you, they eventually should be able to complete them as quickly as you did.

Now it's time to go back and pick up some of the information you completed in chapters 3 and 4. To establish your delegation program, you need to create a grid of tasks, skills, and people. This is a key step in building a successful delegation program.

5

For each task, complete the following chart. Fill in the names of your employees on the lines provided. In the left-hand column, list all the skills, personality traits, aptitudes, etc., that you believe are required to complete the task. In order of their match to each of those skills, rank your employees with 1 being the top rank.

Task Skills Requirements

TASK _____

Employee Names

_____ _____ _____

Skills:

A. _____
B. _____
C. _____
D. _____
E. _____
F. _____
G. _____
H. _____
I. _____

The following chart is a sample for you to follow:

Sample Task Skills Requirements

TASK Weekly Inventory _____

	Employee Names		
	Mary	Tom	Teresa
SKILLS:			
A. Accuracy	1	3	2
B. Math	1	2	3

(continued)

Sample Task Skills Requirements (concluded)

TASK Weekly Inventory

SKILLS:	Mary	Tom	Teresa
	Employee Names		
C. Handwriting	2	3	1
D. Product knowledge	2	1	3
E. Patience	3	2	1

In this example, Mary probably should be your first choice for doing the weekly inventory if she has the time. She has the lowest total score (which in this case is the best) and ranks strongest or at least average in four of the five categories. Of course, if patience is your most important priority, you might want to reconsider using Mary.

If you believe patience is of the greatest importance, you can weight the average. For example, you might decide that everything is equal except patience. Perhaps you believe patience is worth 50 percent more than any other characteristic. In this case, you would add another category that would also be called patience and assign values of 0.5, 1.0, and 1.5 respectively, instead of 1, 2, or 3. That adds the 50 percent difference into your rating system.

This approach is not foolproof. It can, however, help clarify priorities in assigning tasks.

Use the information you developed in Chapter 3 to determine the requirements of each task and the information from Chapter 4 to determine the skills and abilities of each employee. Keep all the data in your files to help you when new tasks need to be assigned in the future.

PUTTING YOUR PLAN INTO ACTION

Now you have got a list of what it takes to do every task and the capabilities of each of your employees. At this point, you are ready to start assigning tasks.

Using the information from your list, take a look back at the six questions in Chapter 4 and determine if your first choice to handle the task will have the time to complete it. If not, you may have to go to your second choice.

Once you have decided which task to assign to what person, you need to prepare the person. Follow these steps to help ensure the smooth implementation of your program:

1. **Write out instructions for each task.** Make sure they are simple and direct and that they cover every aspect of the task. To gain your employee's acceptance in taking on the task, you need to make it as easy as possible for the employee to get started and to know how to complete the task properly. Written instructions provide start-up information and a reference to help the employee continue doing the task until he or she is completely comfortable with it.

2. **Meet with the employee and review the instructions.** Make sure he or she understands clearly what is expected. Invite questions to clarify any points of concern.

3. **Establish criteria for evaluating each task** (see Chapter 6). Let the employee know what those criteria are. Be open to discussion on these points; your employee may have some good ideas for different and possibly more meaningful evaluation criteria.

4. **Create a contingency plan.** Be prepared for the employee who lacks time to get the task done when needed, for the employee who doesn't understand clearly what has to be done, and for the employee who doesn't have the ability or skill to do the task properly. Your contingency plan could include.

- Turning the task over to your second choice
- Completing the task yourself
- Seeking some other way to do the task
- Seeking some other task that would accomplish the same or similar results

Finally, create one last chart—one that allows you to keep track of who is responsible for what—so that duties are clearly defined.

Task Responsibility

TASK	NAME	DATE ASSIGNED
_____	_____	_____
_____	_____	_____
_____	_____	_____
_____	_____	_____
_____	_____	_____
_____	_____	_____
_____	_____	_____
_____	_____	_____
_____	_____	_____
_____	_____	_____
_____	_____	_____
_____	_____	_____
_____	_____	_____
_____	_____	_____
_____	_____	_____
_____	_____	_____
_____	_____	_____

5

Chapter 5 Checkpoints

✓ Set up your time log to determine how much time each task requires.

✓ For each task you plan to delegate, create a chart listing the necessary tasks and match those tasks to the skills and abilities of your employees.

✓ Select an employee (as your first choice) for each task you plan to delegate.

✓ Develop a contingency plan for each task you plan to delegate.

✓ Set up a reminder system to check on employees.

✓ Create written instructions for each task and review them with the employee.

CHAPTER

6 | Evaluating Your Plan

This chapter will help you to:

- Monitor your delegation assignments.
- Monitor the performance or results of your delegation.
- Evaluate your delegation assignments continually.

Carol Swam works in the marketing department of a real estate development firm. She has established her first delegation program. She has followed the instructions in this book and now has three subordinates in her department doing new tasks. For the first time, Carol can take the time to plan future activities for her department.

Since she started her plan several months ago, a couple of problems have occurred. Some of her employees have asked about swapping assignments. One wants to change the procedures as well. One employee has not lived up to expectations, and Carol is concerned about having to reassign work or even take it back and do it herself.

Carol needs a tool to monitor the effectiveness of her delegation program. ∎

■ Questions to Consider

1. What should Carol do to ensure the effectiveness of her delegation program?

_____

_____

_____

2. How can Carol avoid slipping back to a nondelegating way of supervision?

_____

_____

_____

MONITORING DELEGATION PROGRAMS

In Chapter 5, you learned how to set up an implementation program. You assigned tasks based on the best possible information available: matching employee skills to task requirements.

In some cases, the match will not work out as well as you think it should. The three most common reasons for this are

1. The task requirements turn out to be different from what you thought they would be, and the employee does not have the requisite skills or abilities.
2. The employee is not as skillful as you thought and is unable to do the task correctly or effectively.
3. The employee dislikes or resents the task and deliberately does a poor job.

Regardless of the reason, the results will be less than you expected. You can start to evaluate the problems by looking back at the assignments themselves. Are they still the most logical choice?

Determine the reasons why each task is not being performed as well as it should be. Complete the following chart to help you do so.

Monitoring Task Delegation

TASK _____

	Yes	No
1. Does the employee appear to clearly understand the task?	___	___
2. Does the employee clearly understand the expected results?	___	___
3. Does the employee have the proper training to complete the task?	___	___
4. Does the employee still have time to do the task properly?	___	___
5. Does the employee have a positive attitude about performing the task?	___	___
6. Is the employee physically capable of performing the task?	___	___
7. Is the employee mentally capable of performing the task?	___	___
8. Has the employee received proper recognition and support from his or her supervisor for doing the task?	___	___

Any no answers should be cause for concern.

MONITORING PERFORMANCE RESULTS

There is a difference between doing a job properly and doing the bare minimum to get by. As a supervisor or manager, you are responsible for the output of your department or unit. Consequently, employees who take the bare-minimum approach can hurt everyone's efforts.

When you assign tasks, you need to define clearly how well the task is being performed. The chart on page 42 is designed to help you monitor performance. Feel free to add any elements that are specific or unique to your needs.

The chart uses a numerical ranking system to help you analyze performance. Since more than one person may be assigned to perform a task at different times, the chart allows you to compare the efforts of different people.

If one person always has performed the task, consider offering someone else the opportunity to perform the task and learn another element of the company's business.

Monitoring Performance Results

TASK _____

1 = Excellent
2 = Good
3 = Acceptable but needs improvement
4 = Unacceptable

	Names of People Assigned to Perform the Task		
1. Task completed on time	_____	_____	_____
2. Task completed properly	_____	_____	_____
3. Work is done efficiently	_____	_____	_____
4. Positive attitude about assignment	_____	_____	_____
5. Willingness to take responsibility for his or her work	_____	_____	_____
6. Has clear understanding of the task	_____	_____	_____
7. Takes pride in taking on responsibilities	_____	_____	_____

Take a look at the performance rankings. Possible results of using this chart may include

- Assigning the task all the time to one person who performs well on all the criteria
- Reassigning tasks to different people
- Restructuring the task so it can be delegated (that is, breaking a task into smaller parts and dividing the work among more employees)
- Helping the individual do certain parts of the task
- Providing additional training to help the person perform the task

Completing the chart should not be a one-sided exercise. Ask employees for their feelings as well. Discuss privately with the employee any less-than-acceptable situations. Ask the employee what he or she feels is the cause of the unacceptable work and what you both can do, as a team, to improve the task.

It is usually unwise to take a task back and do it yourself. Such action demonstrates a lack of faith in and support for the employee. If an employee feels unable or incompetent to handle the task and suggests you take it back, you might consider doing so on an interim basis. Your company is still counting on you, and the work must be done.

6

CONTINUAL EVALUATION OF TASKS

Once a task is assigned and the work appears acceptable or better, do not assume things will always continue on an even keel. A variety of things can occur that may affect how well the delegated task continues to be done on a long-term basis.

You also should expect your employees to show continued improvement in doing new tasks. Improvement is part of their learning process. For example, after teaching an employee how to perform a task you may find that within two weeks the work is acceptable and the employee can do it alone. You feel, based on your own experience and that of other employees in the company, that the employee should be doing a good to excellent job within six weeks. At the end of six weeks, you find no improvement. The key is to stay on top of employee performance on an ongoing basis—to make sure there is improvement. The chart on page 44 is designed to help accomplish *ongoing* performance.

In the left-hand column, fill in the time periods appropriate for your company and the task. You might start in days or weeks and then move to a monthly or quarterly time period. Your chart should cover the period of time you think it takes to perform the task at an excellent level.

In the right-hand column, next to the time period, fill in the criteria or characteristics that show where performance should be at that time. In a sense, this chart is an extended job description for one particular facet of the job.

Use this chart as a comparative tool. Is the employee where he or she should be at a particular point in time? Use the Monitoring Performance Results chart (see p. 42) along with employee interviews to determine reasons the employee may not be at the optimum performance level.

Ongoing Performance

TASK _____

Time Period	Level of Performance
_____	_____
_____	_____
_____	_____
_____	_____
_____	_____
_____	_____
_____	_____
_____	_____

Chapter 6 Checkpoints

✓ Define exactly what is expected of each employee in performing a delegated task.

✓ Monitor each employee's performance in handling delegated tasks on an ongoing basis.

✓ If tasks are not performed properly, take steps to determine why.

✓ For improperly performed tasks, develop an action plan to accomplish them correctly.

✓ Monitor performance over a period of time to make sure there is continued improvement.

7 | Developing New Employee Skills

This chapter will help you to:

- Test employee capabilities.
- Get employees to accept new tasks.
- Develop new employee skills.

As a supervisor at a software development and manufacturing company, Van Lljenski knew he needed to upgrade the skills of his employees. Changes in technology and methods necessitated the constant improvement of his employees' skills. New responsibilities and methods frequently were assigned to Van. His challenge was to make sure that his employees could keep up with those changes and learn new skills as needed to accomplish their work. He also had to be concerned with employees accepting new methods and new responsibilities.

Van is looking for ways to test the limits of his employees and to help them develop new skills to perform their jobs as effectively as possible. ■

■ Questions to Consider

1. How can Van test his employees' capabilities?

_____

_____

_____

2. How can Van gain his employees' acceptance of new tasks?

_____

_____

_____

7

TESTING EMPLOYEE CAPABILITIES

Before delegating tasks, be sure that your employees are capable of doing those tasks.

In Chapter 4, you learned how to test employee knowledge, desire, and general capabilities to handle assignments. The purpose was to determine how good a match you could make between the employee's general aptitude and the requirements of the task.

In order to test employee capabilities, you must know what the job requires now or will require in the future.

In as much detail as possible, outline in the following chart the skills that are needed now and in the future to perform the task you wish to delegate. List those tasks in the left-hand column.

In the right-hand column, indicate the skill level of the employee. This will help you to identify areas where the employee needs help. Consider discussing this chart with the employee to make sure your opinions are accurate and are shared by the employee.

Employee Proficiency Scale

Skill Rankings for Employees

1 = Excellent

2 = Good

3 = Adequate

4 = Needs assistance

EMPLOYEE NAME _____

TASK _____

Skills Required Now	This Employee's Level of Proficiency	Skills Likely to Be Required in the Future

Be as specific as possible. For example, if the task currently requires excellent word processing skills, it is likely that part of the work will soon require more advanced computer knowledge. Try to determine as best as possible what new skills will be needed. Then go back to your evaluations from chapters 4 and 6 to see which employee is best suited to the task in question.

If an employee lacks the necessary skill to perform a task, you have two choices:

- Don't delegate the work to that employee.
- Provide the training needed so the employee will be capable of doing the work.

The second option is generally more desirable so long as the employee has the aptitude to do the task and has the willingness to learn how to do the task. If your company has a training department, use their help in developing needed employee skills.

GETTING EMPLOYEES TO ACCEPT NEW TASKS

Once you have decided to assign a task:

- Do not take the task back unless absolutely necessary. To do so can be demoralizing to employees who are trying their best. It also can serve employees as an escape from learning how to do the task in the first place. Employees must assume they will have to learn how to do the work you have assigned in the best possible manner they can.

- Check employees' performances periodically. Make sure they are learning what is needed to do the task properly.

- Encourage employees to make their own decisions about how to do their tasks better. Rather than imposing your ideas on them, let your employees see whether they can find solutions to their task problems. There are two important reasons for doing this: (1) Employees may come up with new ideas or methods that work better for them than those imposed by their supervisor. (2) Employees are more likely to use and retain solutions they find than solutions that are imposed on them.

- Challenge your employees to do the best job they can. Appeal to their sense of pride and accomplishment and take advantage of any available company-sponsored incentive programs.

- Involve your employees in setting performance objectives for themselves. It is much easier for employees to reach goals they have helped set.

- Explain how delegated tasks and their efforts fit into company objectives as a whole. It is much easier to motivate employees who see the results of their work and the impact it may have on others than to motivate employees who see an isolated task and who may not understand its relevance.

Use the Monitoring Delegated Tasks chart to help an employee who is resisting a delegated task or who is unsure of how to handle the task. To help you fill in the chart, a sample version is shown first.

Sample Monitoring Delegated Tasks

Task:	To complete the inventory update form and enter it into the central computer system daily.
Measurement Criteria:	1. Understanding the form.
	2. Knowing the part numbering system and where the inventory number is located.
	3. Accuracy of data entered on the form.
	4. Proper entry of form data to central computer.
Action Steps:	1. Review the forms with employee.
	2. Review the part numbering system with the employee.
	3. Review where part numbers are located.
	4. Conduct a brief test with the employee on part numbering system and location of part numbers by asking the employee to locate and retrieve specific parts.
	5. Check accuracy on a daily basis for several weeks. For any inaccuracies, ask employee to suggest solution to prevent them in the future.
	6. Teach employee how to enter data into the central computer system. Have employee print out entries to check accuracy against the original form.
Follow-up Plan:	Weeks 1–2: Check results daily.
	Weeks 3–8: Check results weekly.
	Every 90 days: Meet with employee and review process and methods to maintain accuracy. Reinforce the reasons this report is important to the company.

7

7

Monitoring Delegated Tasks

Task:

Measurement
Criteria:

Action Steps:

Follow-up Plan:

PROMOTING EMPLOYEE GROWTH

One of the objectives of delegating work is to develop employee skills. When employees lack necessary skills, they can drag down productivity and may feel frustrated in their efforts to be productive workers.

As you delegate tasks, make a list of skills that employees seem to lack. (You can use the chart that follows as a starting point.) The skills probably will fall into one of three categories:

1. Basic skills such as language, math, or reading.
2. Attitudinal/personality traits such as attention to detail, patience, or empathy.
3. Higher job task skills such as knowing how to use a piece of machinery or understanding basic accounting.

All of these can be addressed with training, although some are easier to improve than others. As you see trends emerging with your employees, determine the areas where they need improvement. Take the steps your-self or with your human resources department to make the necessary improvements.

Employee Skills Improvement

Employee Name   **Needs Improvement In**

_____   _____

_____   _____

_____   _____

_____   _____

_____   _____

_____   _____

_____   _____

_____   _____

_____   _____

7

Chapter 7 Checkpoints

✓ Test employee knowledge before assigning skills.

✓ Rank employee skills in relation to task requirements.

✓ Identify key areas where individuals and your department need to improve.

✓ Involve your employees in the process of determining how to do a given task most efficiently.

✓ Make a point of developing new employee skills as their need becomes apparent.

8 | Delegation and the Supportive Supervisor

This chapter will help you to:

- Understand the role of a supervisor or manager in the delegation process.
- Identify employee needs as they relate to delegation.
- Work more closely with your manager or supervisor.

As a supervisor with a fair amount of experience at a Big Eight accounting firm, Janelle Littlejohn developed the habit of delegating work as much as possible. In most cases, the work was done well and her employees responded enthusiastically to the opportunities she provided them. In some cases, however, her employees did not do as well as they could; in others, after some period of time, performance declined with the new tasks.

Janelle's superior is beginning to wonder if Janelle is delegating too much work or if she is delegating the wrong tasks to the wrong people. Janelle is also concerned. ■

Questions to Consider

1. Does Janelle understand her role in the delegation process?

_____

_____

_____

2. What can Janelle do to be more supportive of her employees?

_____

_____

_____

3. What can Janelle do to gain more support from her supervisor?

_____

_____

_____

THE ROLE OF THE SUPERVISOR

Delegating work to others involves many key decisions. Which tasks do you delegate? To whom do you delegate? When do you delegate? How is delegated work evaluated?

In addition, the human element plays a role in the delegation process. As a supervisor, you need to support your employees in their efforts to learn, develop, and apply new skills and to help them to advance their careers.

Take the following test to see how you do in supporting your employees with delegated work.

Do You Support Your Employees with Delegated Work?

	Always	Sometimes	Rarely
1. I delegate work as much as possible.	____	____	____
2. I delegate every task that reasonably can be delegated.	____	____	____
3. I carefully match tasks to the appropriate people.	____	____	____
4. I try to challenge employees and expand their capabilities.	____	____	____
5. I provide careful training for a delegated task.	____	____	____
6. I test the employee's knowledge to make sure he or she understands the task.	____	____	____
7. I provide coaching and assistance as needed while the employee performs the task.	____	____	____
8. I am available to answer questions as needed.	____	____	____
9. I am patient with employees learning new tasks.	____	____	____
10. I avoid harshly criticizing an employee who is handling a delegated task.	____	____	____
11. I give the employee a second chance (or more if needed and time permits).	____	____	____
12. I ask for feedback on how the employee feels about doing the task.	____	____	____
13. I encourage employees to be creative and come up with new ways to do the task.	____	____	____

8

Give yourself 3 points for each always, 2 points for each sometimes, and 1 point for each rarely.

If your score is over 30, you are a relatively sensitive and caring supervisor who wants your employees to succeed. If your score is between 20 and 30, you have some good ideas and good intentions but you need to get more involved with your employees in helping them improve their skills. If your score is under 20, rethink your role as a supervisor. Delegation is a critical part of supervision, and you may want to look back at your general handling of employees as well as how and why you delegate work.

DELEGATION AND IDENTIFYING EMPLOYEE NEEDS

As a supervisor, you have the following needs:

- Producing the work assigned to you
- Coordinating and supervising your staff
- Determining which tasks to assign to which people
- Helping employees to improve their skills and perform their tasks as effectively and efficiently as possible
- Providing support and feedback to employees
- Coaching employees as needed
- Evaluating employees' performance

Employees also have needs, and they vary from person to person. As a supervisor, you should make the utmost effort to be sensitive to those needs.

Employees often want to know "What's in it for me?" when they are asked to perform a delegated task. The answer to their question can include any of the following:

- Pride and responsibility
- Career advancement
- Pay raise

- Public recognition
- Increased power and influence
- Acquisition of new skills

Use the following chart to determine employee motivations and needs. Wait until you have assigned a task and have seen how well the employee handles it before completing this chart.

Determining Employee Needs

Employee name _____

Task _____

Performance level of employee (circle one):

Excellent   Good   Fair   Needs improvement

If "fair" or "needs improvement," what are the most likely causes? (Lacks training, doesn't understand, doesn't like to do it, etc.)

Ask the employee for an explaination of why his or her performance is not up to your standards. List the top three reasons given by the employee:

1. _____

2. _____

3. _____

8

After you have identified a problem, complete the chart below. List the problem in the left-hand column. In the right-hand column, write out your planned course of action. Your plan may include assigning the task to someone else or disciplining the employee if the reasons are attitudinal in nature.

```
┌─────────────────────────────────────────────────────────────┐
│                        Action Plan                            │
│                                                               │
│   Employee name _____          │
│                                                               │
│   Task _____          │
│                                                               │
│                                           Plan of Action      │
│                  Problem              (including date to implement) │
│                                                               │
│                                                               │
│                                                               │
│                                                               │
│                                                               │
│                                                               │
│                                                               │
│                                                               │
│                                                               │
│                                                               │
└─────────────────────────────────────────────────────────────┘
```

WORKING MORE CLOSELY WITH YOUR OWN SUPERIOR

Delegation is a part of the job of supervisor. It is one of your duties. Most supervisors are accountable for delegation as well on other managerial and supervisory performance skills. In addition, you clearly need support and a good relationship with your *own* superior.

Here are some tips to help you build a better relationship with your supervisor or manager and gain support for your efforts:

1. Keep your supervisor informed. Let the supervisor know that you are delegating certain tasks and to whom they are delegated.

2. Keep your supervisor apprised of how your delegation efforts are going. Which employees are responsive and which are not? Which tasks are being handled well and which are not?

3. Ask your supervisor for help when needed. Your supervisor may be able to offer excellent advice about which tasks to delegate and how to handle the delegation process.

4. Ask for your supervisor's feedback as well as advice. Find out how well you are doing as a delegator.

5. Make sure you have your supervisor's support for your efforts. You want to avoid employee end runs to your manager or supervisor.

8

Chapter 8 Checkpoints

✓ Take a personal interest in how well your employees handle delegated tasks.

✓ Provide support, guidance, and instruction.

✓ Ask employees how they feel about handling newly delegated tasks.

✓ Involve your manager or supervisor by informing him or her of your delegation decisions and asking for input when needed.

9 | The Positive Results of Delegation

This chapter will help you to:

- Appreciate the positive results gained by delegating work to others.

Mark Johnson's employer, a plastics company, recently cut back the number of supervisors as a cost-savings measure and asked each remaining supervisor to take on additional work. The only way Mark can handle the new work load is by delegating as much of it as possible and as quickly as possible.

In the past, Mark has found that in some cases it is still faster and certainly more reliable to do a job himself. Delegation takes time. Employees need to be motivated to take on more work, and often they need to be taught what to do, how to do it, and then closely monitored to make sure the task is done right. ■

■ Question to Consider

1. Mark sees the obvious advantages to his employees of having work delegated to them. But what's in it for Mark?

_____

_____

_____

POSITIVE RESULTS FOR THE SUPERVISOR

Delegation requires a lot of up front effort. Done properly, there are many clear results that will make your life easier as a supervisor and that will help you advance your own career.

Time. Without delegating work, most supervisors would be overwhelmed. By definition, a supervisor "supervises"—tasks, people, or both. It is good "management" of your time to delegate work whenever possible.

Sense of accomplishment. Work gets done—more work than most supervisors could ever do alone. Your output is maximized by delegating.

9

Pride. Helping others improve their skills and learn new tasks creates pride in the accomplishments your employees achieve.

Recognition. Good performance often leads to recognition by superiors and other employees. Delegating work often creates recognition because of increased output and the development of people skills.

New methods and techniques. Assigning work to subordinates may stimulate their thinking. In their efforts to save time, reduce effort, etc., they may create or discover new ways to handle the task. A new method might turn out to be a tremendous time/effort/cost saver for the company. A fresh perspective may cause you to take another look at whether the task is still needed or useful. Subordinates who have never performed a task have no vested interest in how that task has been done. They frequently can bring a fresh perspective that will change and improve the way the task is performed.

Improved management skills. Your own career as a supervisor or manager depends on ever-improving management skills. Delegating work is one of the most difficult and most critical skills leading to success.

POSITIVE RESULTS FOR THE COMPANY

Delegating work also provides the company with some positive results.

Greater efficiency. By managing the people and processes in your areas of responsibility, you match the tasks to the people. You help ensure the most efficient use of talent, which in turn results in greater productivity.

Finding and developing new supervisory talent. Delegation of work may involve several employees. Their ability to handle new challenges or respond to difficult situations may help identify new leadership talent. Growing companies are always in need of new supervisory talent. Therefore it is an extremely positive reflection on you when people in your department are recognized for their efforts. If very little work or responsibility is given to your subordinates, no one will ever know what they are capable of doing.

A way to test your overall management skills. Because the primary skills of management and supervision are managing people and processes—not doing individual tasks—your ability to delegate work becomes a key measurement by which your manager or supervisor will evaluate how well you are doing.

More stable workforce. Employees who are challenged and recognized for their efforts are more likely to stay on the job and continue to grow. Supervisors who do not entrust any responsibility to their subordinates are inviting frustration and a lack of interest.

POSITIVE RESULTS FOR THE EMPLOYEE

Delegating work provides positive results for the employee too.

Sense of accomplishment. Employees who are entrusted with new responsibilities take pride in their ability to handle the work.

Sense of career development.   Employees working under supervisors who entrust work to them see a company that is employee-oriented and happy to help employees improve themselves.

Greater job interest.   Variety and change on the job can greatly stimulate interest. Greater interest usually means higher productivity. Giving employees new challenges often leads to a renewed interest in their work and a desire to expand their knowledge and improve their skills to an even greater degree.

Pride!   Learning new skills and impressing one's boss can instill a lot of pride. Giving your subordinates that opportunity through delegation of work can help them take greater pride in their contribution to the company.

POSITIVE RESULTS FOR THE CUSTOMER

All businesses and organizations have customers. Delegating work affects the organization's customers as well as the organization itself in positive ways.

Lower costs.   The most efficient use of talent by your organization means lower costs and better value for your customers. Customers will not have to pay for inefficiencies caused by supervisors who want to do everything themselves and, consequently, turn out fewer products or services, and those of poorer quality.

Greater access to information and help.   Being the only one who knows how something is done does not make you irreplaceable to the company. It encourages your company to find someone to replace you who is more open to helping other employees grow on the job.

Customers want help and information as quickly as possible. If you are the only one who can provide it and you are on vacation, out sick, or just too busy to respond, your company runs the risk of losing customers. Well-run organizations try to have multiple resources for information, products, and services. Well-trained subordinates, therefore, are invaluable to you.

Reliability.   Customers want to know that you deliver a consistent level of service and quality. Delegating work to some extent requires standardizing methods and ideas; the result is that customers see consistent quality no matter who they talk to in your organization. Knowledge is shared and a smoother-running business is the result.

Chapter 9 Checkpoints

✓ Take a big picture view of your role as a supervisor and avoid getting bogged down in details that should be the concern of your employees.

✓ Focus on the importance of maximizing efficiency and productivity.

✓ Be open to innovation and new ideas that result from delegating work.

✓ Take pride in seeing your subordinates develop new skills, including leadership.

Post-Test

You have just taken another step in your professional development by completing *Delegation Skills*.

This post-test is provided to reinforce the material you have just covered. If you have difficulty with any question, go back to the book to review key concepts.

1. List the ways your subordinates will benefit from your use of delegation.

   _____

   _____

   _____

   _____

2. Identify the primary reasons that supervisors and managers find it difficult to delegate work to other people.

   _____

   _____

   _____

3. What can you do to overcome the obstacles you identified in Question 2.

   _____

   _____

   _____

4. List the questions you should ask yourself when deciding whether a specific task should or should not be delegated.

   _____

   _____

   _____

5. List the questions you should ask yourself when determining whether a particular person is capable of handling a delegated task.

   _____

   _____

   _____

6. To establish a successful delegation program, it is helpful to create a grid of _____, _____, and _____.

7. What steps should you follow to ensure the smooth implementation of your delegation plan?

_____

_____

_____

8. List the most common reasons that a supervisor's matches of employee skills to task requirements may result in failure.

_____

_____

_____

9. What questions should you ask yourself when determining why a delegated task is not being performed well?

_____

_____

_____

10. What role should your supervisor play in your effort to delegate work to subordinates?

_____

_____

_____

11. Identify the positive customer-oriented results of delegating tasks to subordinates.

_____

_____

_____

Business Skills Express Series

This growing series of books addresses a broad range of key business skills and topics to meet the needs of employees, human resource departments, and training consultants.

To obtain information about these and other Business Skills Express books, please call Irwin Professional Publishing toll free at: 1-800-634-3966.

Effective Performance Management
ISBN   1-55623-867-3

Hiring the Best
ISBN   1-55623-865-7

Writing that Works
ISBN   1-55623-856-8

Customer Service Excellence
ISBN   1-55623-969-6

Writing for Business Results
ISBN   1-55623-854-1

Powerful Presentation Skills
ISBN   1-55623-870-3

Meetings that Work
ISBN   1-55623-866-5

Effective Teamwork
ISBN   1-55623-880-0

Time Management
ISBN   1-55623-888-6

Assertiveness Skills
ISBN   1-55623-857-6

Motivation at Work
ISBN   1-55623-868-1

Overcoming Anxiety at Work
ISBN   1-55623-869-X

Positive Politics at Work
ISBN   1-55623-879-7

Telephone Skills at Work
ISBN   1-55623-858-4

Managing Conflict at Work
ISBN   1-55623-890-8

The New Supervisor: Skills for Success
ISBN   1-55623-762-6

**The *Americans with Disabilities Act*:
What Supervisors Need to Know**
ISBN   1-55623-889-4

Managing the Demands of Work and Home
ISBN   0-7863-0221-6

Effective Listening Skills
ISBN   0-7863-0102-4

Goal Management at Work
ISBN   0-7863-0225-9

Positive Attitudes at Work
ISBN   0-7863-0100-8

Supervising the Difficult Employee
ISBN   0-7863-0219-4

Cultural Diversity in the Workplace
ISBN   0-7863-0125-2

Managing Organizational Change
ISBN   0-7863-0162-7

Negotiating for Business Results
ISBN   0-7863-0114-7

Practical Business Communication
ISBN   0-7863-0227-5

High Performance Speaking
ISBN   0-7863-0222-4

Delegation Skills
ISBN   0-7863-0105-9

Coaching Skills: A Guide for Supervisors
ISBN   0-7863-0220-8

Customer Service and the Telephone
ISBN   0-7863-0224-0

Creativity at Work
ISBN   0-7863-0223-2

Total Quality Selling
ISBN   0-7863-0274-7

Effective Interpersonal Relationships
ISBN   0-7863-0255-0

The Participative Leader
ISBN   0-7863-0252-6

Building Customer Loyalty
ISBN   0-7863-0253-4

Getting and Staying Organized
ISBN   0-7863-0254-2

Business Etiquette
ISBN   0-7863-0273-9

Skill Maintenance

You will get the most out of the training you have just completed if you reinforce your skills at regular intervals. This checklist will help you practice and maintain your skills.

USING THE CHECKLIST

Write today's date below. Using this date as a base, fill in the three dates on top of the column below. Put a reminder in your calendar to return to and complete this checklist on those dates. Use the chapter reference column to review material for any item checked no.

Today's date: _____

	Date ___ 3 Months		Date ___ 6 Months		Date ___ 1 Year		
	Yes	No	Yes	No	Yes	No	Chapter Reference
1. I understand why delegating work is so vitally important.							1
2. I consciously work to overcome the obstacles to delegating tasks.							2
3. I prioritize my work on a regular basis to determine which tasks I can delegate.							3
4. I maintain an updated list of tasks that can be delegated.							3
5. I know the strengths and weaknesses of my employees when delegating tasks.							4
6. I've created a delegation plan for myself.							5
7. I continually evaluate how delegated tasks are carried out.							6
8. I assign tasks that help employees develop new skills.							7
9. I try to match employee needs to the tasks I delegate.							7
10. I see the positive results of delegating tasks to others.							8